More praise for *If Moth&*

"Patterson's first full-length collection of poems is a history, a feminist revolt, and a personal unraveling of Mormonism, ancestors, family, and identity. These poems articulate conflict, secret narratives, homage, and questions to those long past who will never respond. From granddaughter to missionary to mother and poet, Patterson gives us poems that enchant, reveal, and document both myth and truth."
—**Trish Hopkinson**, author of *Footnote*; recipient of awards from the Utah State Poetry Society and Utah Arts Festival

"'I'm Mormon the way stars—rubbed out at noon ... still burn': Dayna Patterson's bold, linguistically pyrotechnic and terribly moving testament to faith renounced and still omnipresent reclaims matriarchy and mitochondrial inheritance, making a chant from the names of Brigham Young's polygamous wives, studying hard for belief through intimate epistolaries to ancestors in a past where polygamy is 'familiar as summer/sweat.' 'The Mormons are coming,' Patterson declares, and she interrogates that ancestral, theological, and gendered onslaught brilliantly through poems of fierce reinvention and homage: 'Our orthodoxy/changed, etched over, effaced//by our palimpsestuous selves.'" —**Bruce Beasley**, author of *All Soul Parts Returned*; recipient of Colorado Prize for Poetry; professor of English at Western Washington University

If MOTHER BRAIDS A WATERFALL

IF MOTHER BRAIDS A WATERFALL

poems by DAYNA PATTERSON

Signature Books | 2020 | Salt Lake City

Cover design by Hailey Romero.

FIRST EDITION | 2020

LIBRARY OF CONGRESS CATALOGING-IN-PUBLICATION DATA

Names: Patterson, Dayna, author.

Title: If mother braids a waterfall / poems by Dayna Patterson.

Description: First edition. | Salt Lake City : Signature Books, 2020. | Summary: "Dayna
                Patterson has produced a book obsessed with motherhood and daughter-
                hood, ancestry, and transition-of home, family, faith, and the narratives woven
                to uphold the Self. In her debut collection of poetry and lyric essay, Patterson
                grapples with a patriarchal and polygamous heritage. After learning about her
                mother's bisexuality, Patterson befriends doubt while simultaneously feeling
                the urge to unearth a feminist theology, one that envisions God the Mother
                taking pride of place at the banquet table"—Provided by publisher.

Identifiers: LCCN 2019050855 (print) | LCCN 2019050856 (ebook) | ISBN 9781560852803
                (paperback) | ISBN 9781560853763 (ebook)

Subjects: LCSH: Church of Jesus Christ of Latter-day Saints—Poetry. | Mothers and
                daughters—Poetry. | God—Motherhood—Poetry. | Motherhood—Religious
                aspects—Poetry. | Mormons—Poetry. | Mormon women—Poetry. | Christian
                poetry. | Feminist poetry. | LCGFT: Poetry.

Classification: LCC PS3616.A8747 I34 2020 (print) | LCC PS3616.A8747 (ebook) |
                DDC 811/.6—dc23

                LC record available at https://lccn.loc.gov/2019050855
                LC ebook record available at https://lccn.loc.gov/2019050856

For my mothers and foremothers

CONTENTS

*I had no saints, so I turned
to my ancestors*

—Susan Elizabeth Howe, *Salt*

BAILEY FAMILY TREE

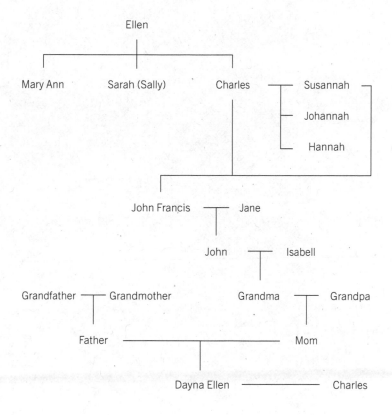

THE MORMONS ARE COMING

Mormons bring a handmade wreath of white mesh, silver ribbon, tinsel sprigs. A cheese-and-potato casserole. An offering of white lilies.

Mormons bring a package of diapers. A green onesie. A purple turtle quilt. They bring a musical mobile that dangles Eeyore, Piglet, Tigger, and Pooh.

They surprise you with a two-foot Christmas tree, white lights, red balls, and a golden star.

They bring cranberry orange walnut bread. Gingerbread. Cinnamon rolls.

They say *I'm sorry for your loss*. They say *Congratulations!* They say *Merry Christmas*.

The Mormons are coming.

They drink eggnog without rum. They drink Ovaltine and Postum. They drink Mountain Dew and Diet Coke in 32 oz. mugs. Energy drinks, yes. Coffee and tea, no. Alcohol, never.

Mormons rake your leaves, weed your weeds, babysit your kid while you go to the hospital to have another kid.

Mormons build monuments of prairie families and covered wagons and handcarts. They hold the weight of family trees and martyrdom and pioneer blood in their cupped palms.

They say *My ancestors knew Joseph Smith. Donated their china for crushing to make the temple's stucco sparkle. Buried their massacred dead at Haun's Mill.*

My husband says *My ancestor was Brigham Young's shoemaker, and there were a lot of little feet to shod.*

I say *My ancestor went to prison for polygamy. 3 wives, 19 sons, 9 daughters. 107 grandchildren.*

Mormons bless their new babies in white, baptize their children in white coveralls and pinafores.

White at their weddings. White in their temples. White when they're laid out in their coffins, an apron of green around their waists.

They wear white undergarments woven with folkloric magic. Bullets repelled. Burns deflected.

Mormons dot hills with electric spires. Nauvoo Temple. Salt Lake Temple. A temple in your neighborhood, brazenly bright.

The Mormons are coming.

They come in the middle of the night when you have a blinding migraine. They come with consecrated olive oil and warm hands and baritone prayers.

They come in the morning and sweep up the crying baby.

They come in the afternoon and feed your cats, your turtles, your birds.

Mormons bring a space blanket. A flashlight with extra batteries. A portable radio.

A case of granola bars. A bucket of wheat. A crate of water.

The Mormons are coming. By car. By bicycle. On foot. They knock on your door. They wear black name tags and glowing faces and shiny hope.

I wore a name tag: *Soeur Kidd, Église de Jésus-Christ des Saint des Derniers Jours.* French in my mouth a mangled nasturtium.

They say *Welcome to the neighborhood.* They say *It's nice to meet you.* They say *See you Sunday.*

Mormon men wear white shirts, dark suits, and power ties. They are clean cut, well-shaven. Mormon women wear dresses or skirts in peach, spring green, lilac. A few rebels wear slacks.

Mormons say *Follow the prophet.* They say *Fathers preside.* They say *Men have priesthood, women have motherhood.*

Mormons gather for Sabbath in low-church chapels. They shush their gigawatt kids, and pass silver plates of torn Wonder Bread, trays of water in thimble-size paper cups.

My daughters ask *Why do only boys pass the sacrament?*

Mormons build a grand conference center with a waterfall welcome mat, a garden roof of native grasses and trees. They build it big enough to park two planes inside, to gather Mormon masses from around the world. They arrange a room of plinths with the bronze busts of their prophets.

My daughters ask *Why are all the statues of men?*

Mormons issue proclamations. A proclamation to wash away polygamy. A proclamation to define the family— marriage between man and woman only.

They say *Families Are Forever*, and paint the words in cursive above their doors like a threshold blessing, a paschal lamb's blood.

The Mormons are coming.

Mormons put up Prop 8 signs. They make calls. They go door to door.

They have practice going door to door.

They say *Hate the sin but not the sinner*. They say *It's a choice*. They say *Gay is okay, just stay celibate*.

And when a daughter, son, aunt, uncle, cousin, best friend, or _____ comes out—

My mother tells me *I'm bisexual*—

I agonize for half a decade's doubt before deciding to leave.

Mormons send priesthood holders. Mormons send sister teachers. Mormons send missionaries.

And when I ask them to stop, they send a card every month.

A card with no return address.

The cards say *It's spring now*.

Summer's here.

Autumn's coming.

ODE TO POLYGAMY

1.
Fact: there's an efficiency to polygamy for spreading
the Alpha-male's seed. And a wife can educate herself,
leave children with sister-wife sitters while she skives off
to medical school or scribbles verse. There's a long

history of polygamy, so it can't be all grotesque. Fact:
popular among vertebrates, especially mammals,
and not something invented by Mormons, it stretches back
centuries, to the Hebrews, Chinese, and Islam's foundations.

Poly*gamy* (many partners) usually means poly*gyny*
(many wives) rather than poly*andry* (many husbands).
In my grandma's parlor sits a carefully-curated poster
with pictures of my three-greats-grandfather, the polygamist,

2.
and his nineteen sons. Grandpa Charles with his billowy white
mustachios, the stately cylinder of his Abe Lincoln hat.
There should be a companion photo showing his
nine daughters, but that portrait, if it exists, doesn't prove

poster-worthy. Polygamy. Husband sharing.
Part-time penis-partaking. Sown and sown and then
—perhaps, the best part?—left alone. Or the worst. Fact:
some sister wives cohabit, split the chore list: First takes kids,

Second cooks meals, Third cleans house. Each with a niche, organized
like a beehive with one king and all those worker-queens,
swapping gossip about their husband's preferences in bed,
while they almanac a rotary schedule for his seed.

3.
Grandma's poster she displays like a bestowal
of jewels. At a Bailey reunion, a third cousin calls out
the question: *How many women did Charles Ramsden marry?*
My grandma yells the correct answer: *Four.* The first

divorced him. The next two he married the same day.
I learn this when I'm seventeen years old, the same age
Hannah was when Grandpa married her, his fourth. I learn this
over the best peach pie I've ever tasted, assaulted

by the tang of peaches from the orchard across the street,
and by the newsflash that my family tree twists, branches,
in ways I wouldn't have guessed; that my genealogy's
complex. Fact: I wouldn't be *me* without *it*.

DEAR GRANDMA

I like the way you bent over to shake your breasts
into your bra, the way you showed
Mom how to do it, the way she
showed me.

And I've learned its comfort,
swells settled in their
cloth cups
with the help of shimmy and gravity.

I wonder if your mother
showed you
and her mother
showed her, this lacy,

intimate knowledge
from one Eve to another,
mother to daughter,
mitochondrial.

How to girl into woman.
How to gather oneself.

MAY DAY

In a western town in the foothills of the Wasatch,
folk still gather on the green adjacent the church
to flower-wreath crown their festival queen.

They come in overalls and scraped-clean boots,
straw hats and hard vowels. They come in cotton
dresses and petal-plaited hair, scrubbed faces

and gleaming hope. They come to watch the young
circle the May pole. Ribbons in primaveral colors
weave, unweave. And county kin surround them

clapping hands, stomping feet, keeping rhythm, this
ancient beat of bloom, harvest, snow, and bloom again,
all hunger and hard times like heavy winter quilts

stowed away in cedar chests, all the cold, for a time,
forgotten in their queen's hummingbird smiles,
in the deep dimples of the dairy farmer's son.

DEAR ELLEN, 1852

1.

Like a moth in autumn,
a flame in a cave, I imagine you
flickering, fading, my ancestress,

great-
     great-
          great-
               great-

grandmother, passer-on of
                    name and faith.

My mother's   mother's
first kin to convert,

          I have a mouth of bees
          hungry for your royal jelly   (miles from the hive), treble
          to tenor ready for ringing   (peals in negative decibels).

                  I know
my feet wouldn't fit your winter
shoes, my waist would burst
your laces. Still,

          I slip on your secondhand cotton,
          whalebone,

               shoehorn into your leather.

2.

Old mother,
                    I searchlight

West Yorkshire, over a century and a half ago,
where you raise daughters, Mary Ann and Sally,
and a young son, Charles,

                    a mill-boy at seven,
two shillings for sweeping scraps, doffing bobbins,
careful in the clatter. Some of those kids lost

fingers. You didn't want him to succumb
to chronic coughs, tuberculosis, breathing in
lint and dust.

                                        I imagine
you wanted to give your children   rivers
without sludge, fluff-free air,
full bellies, enough to hush

the grumbling. Maybe you aspired to education, some XYZs
to their ABCs. Or apprenticeship in a prosperous trade—law
in lieu of glassworks. You probably longed for

                                        space
room to flex
                    flightless wings.

                    And better marriage prospects,
men with more class than your last   tooth and bruise

wages drunk   whiskey prints on your wrist   shattered
scraps of china.   Even though you'd left him,

the possibility of return   curdled.

3.
So when the Mormons came
offering new doctrine
like a Golden West—

        the resurrected Christ
        preaching in the Americas; Joseph Smith
        a mouthpiece
        for God; golden plates translated
        into a second Bible; visits from angels
        and the spillway of heaven

        opened,
        these bright nuggets sluiced,
        sparking   life   light   promise

—what part of you could resist?

JOSEPH SMITH'S DEATH MASK

Lacking time travel, this pale imprint
is perhaps as close as I can get

to a ghost, the slope of nose prominent,
chin cleft, broad forehead,

and those sensuous lips
like a woman's. They almost-smile, serene, withhold

a trove that slant rhymes eternity

> (stories hearth-spun for family
> gathered around his boyhood, gifted
> treasure-seeker, angel see-er, farmhand
> to famous God-talker, first
> one wife and then all that followed
> furtively, three masonic knocks
> and aproned waists, mummies
> with papyrus funerary texts signed Abraham,
> *not* Book of the Dead, horses thundering
> Pre-Columbian America)

an imperturbable penetralia, those shut lips,
prison of secrets, plaster-cast tomb, prophet tome,

(Oh enigma whose shrouded legacy
I shuck, charisma seeping a century)

those closed lips
sealed like so many plates,

golden   shining   silent   still   stilled   mum   shush

HYRUM SMITH'S DEATH MASK

I'd rather interact with a life mask,
plaster imprint of living flesh, cold wet
pressed up against warm dry
skin, eyelids closed

temporarily, breath held

released at last.
                        At the new
Church History Museum, a stranger
points out the pocked flesh
next to Hyrum's left
nostril, little volcano
where bullet Vesuviused

through. The image haunts me
more than seer stone's honey
striations, more than First Vision
versions—all nine—wall mounted
by theater's exit. More than my exit
from the faith of ancestors
whose dotted line I finger-follow
on the pioneer interactive map
from England across the Atlantic to
Louisiana to Utah. Their faces bright
on bright.
                        These faces sear:
seer and brother
who brothered on
past the end. The end that stoppered
their glow behind glass.

DEAR ELLEN, 1855

On the clipper ship *Charles Buck*
I wonder if you carried a spider
in a walnut shell for luck, or if your new faith

was enough. Like a pail brimming spring
water, I imagine you overfull, clear,
perhaps sloshing a little here and there,

from Liverpool to New Orleans,
as mothers dropped stiff
bundles into the hungry Atlantic.

Did you keep your children
close, below deck, sewing tents
and wagon covers for the trek?

At least you and yours were whole—
until Mary Ann tumbled from the wagon.
The oxen pulled the first wheel

over her chest, puncturing lung,
the hind wheel over her jaw, shattering bone.
Did her disfigured face make you ask,

What are you up to, God
Almighty? *The Lord gave,
and the Lord hath taken away . . .*

Late September when you arrived,
pitched a tent in desert
needlegrass and basin wildrye. Here, rumors

swarmed. Did you see Brigham's
executive mansion, just finished? The beehive
atop the Widow's Watch,

adobe walls calcimined
pale yellow? Were any drops of lucid water left
in the pail you carried

caged in your ribs?
I wonder if regret was a meal you ate
then, bitter dish, with autumn spinning

fool's gold, the Wasatch mountains
snipped with snow, winter
lumbering around the corner.

BRIGHAM'S WIVES

Miriam and Mary Ann and Lucy Ann and Augusta and Harriet and Clarissa and Emily and Clarissa and Louisa and Eliza and Elizabeth and Clarissa and Rebecca and Diana and Susanne and Olive and Mary Ann and Margaret and Mary and Emmeline and Mary and Margaret and Olive and Emily and Martha and Ellen and Jemima and Abigail and Phebe and Cynthia and Mary and Rhoda and Zina and Amy and Mary Ellen and Julia and Abigail and Mary Ann and Naamah and Nancy and Jane and Lucy and Mary Jane and Sarah and Eliza and Mary and Eliza and Catherine and Harriet and Amelia and Mary and Ann Eliza and Elizabeth and Lydia and Hannah and

DEAR GRANDPA

Every time we greeted
you'd pinch my cheek
hard, too hard for the tease
you meant it to be. I'd cry
and you'd laugh it off. I braced
myself for your fingers' vice
Sundays at church. The red of my cheek
a one-sided blush. Then one day, grown to a teen,
before you had the chance I grabbed your face and pinched
hard as I could, a laugh on my lips, a decade's bruises to avenge.
You never tried it again. And although you've been gone years, I remember
your face snagged with surprise: this grandgirl clacking her claws.

DEAR ELLEN, 1863

Tell me, Old Mother, of that day in November,

of your son's double wedding—the girl he'd courted
on one arm, the girl he'd just met on the other. Did he share

with you his recurring dream, heavy

as prophecy? Did you join them on the road south
to the Salt Lake Endowment House, rejoice as they knelt

at the altar to be sealed? On that autumn day,

did aspen leaves shudder and bigtooth maples snap
bloody flags? Or did you trudge to the nuptials

in feet of snow? Maybe you thought you'd raised a saint

compared to his Pa—he'd be twice the man.
No mangled lips. No doors torn from hinges.

Did Charles tell you of the elder's promise: two wives

to replace the bride who'd ditched him? When she left,
did you break as he broke? When he married, did you mend

as he mended? What machinery was set in motion

in your heart? All I have to go on is *his* diary, *his* words.
Consider this my standing invitation. Dear Ancestress, Matriarch,

Root: I want to taste your song, to hear your salt.

CONTRAILS

The planes fly green today, their wings
washed with foamy antifreeze and salt crumbs
dissolved to a dish soap slick. From up here,

clouds look like waves of milk,
or jet skied snow, or white cotton candy stretched
round Mount Rainier's superb surprise.

What is the Truth? I wish I could tell
where you are, Grandfather. These clouds
put me in mind of a gentle, pearlescent heaven,

soften thoughts of oblivion. When neurons
hush to silent, when the multiple pulsing
frequencies still, where goes the you

you once were? Did you fragment, leave
pieces in our memories like glowing stones?
Does any part of you hibernate in your body's carapace?

Or did you move on—is there an *on*?—board the one-
way flight with no return? You
were a caricature of good, Dickensian in your extreme

angelic. You visited prisoners, cared for the poor.
Paid a stubborn granddaughter's piano lessons,
paid to wire straight her chaos of teeth.

I don't know about Truth, but I do know
you mapped new paths of inclusion,
ways to navigate this world's chill

shell of blue, leaving us sublime
lines chalking the sky.

GRANDMOTHER

My girl tumbles off the curb
and there you are after twenty-five years—
a *darn-a-luck* on my tongue

I sneeze in a room alone
and there you are, too,
a self-served *Bless me*

And here you are tucked behind my eyes,
bent over a rainbow on a frame,
your mouth full of sibilant laughter

Your crone magic made mermaid fins
of afghans and safety pins,
unicorn coves from sheets and sofas,
quilts from scraps patched and patterned
warm to dream under

You were a kitchen with swinging
doors, cinnamon toast, homemade
raspberry jam on buttered bread,
split pea soup, the kind a kid wanted
after a week of stomach flu

You were a slender white wand
measuring out a hymn, a song that
slid into the loose pockets of our childhood

And when Mom left, what could we do
but give you her name

AFTER THE DIVORCE

The porcelain dolls at Christmas
that Mom set, painted, and sewed
were saying, I'm sorry.

The four-hour trips from Hailey to Logan
and back again every other weekend
were saying, I'm sorry.

The cupboards full of our favorite food
(she couldn't afford),
all the Mountain Dew, Funyuns,
were saying, I'm sorry.

The balloons, jelly beans, flowers.
The perfume, peach pie, hours
of saying, I'm sorry, so, so sorry.

All fire in her bones,
marrowed with regret.
In spite of this, we loved her.

HIPPOCAMPUS

The female seahorse
tendrils her tail around his,
brings him close in their morning dance.

Later, she'll close the distance
between their bellies,
and pump his pouch full of eggs.

There they dwell, hatch, grow, until,
body bucking, he spurts the fry
into the surrounding sea.

Who decides who is female, male?
Mother, Father? When she left,
we were three, two, and one, all in diapers. Fry

measure less than half an inch,
the length of a fingernail,
yet from dad they have enough

to drift, wrap their tails earnestly
around seagrass, sift for shrimp, and secure
mates, homes of their own.

Dad, I want to give you a gold trophy
of Hippocampus, a blue ribbon
embroidered with an orange seahorse.

The way our lives unfolded,
when we look close
at one of those pregnant males,

there should be a little badge with
your image
over the button of his heart.

GROWING UP IN A BOOKSTORE

My first steps are watched over
by sad-eyed Brontës.

On hands and knees I buff away
black scuffs from butter-colored wood.

At Christmas, my fingers learn
the perfect shape of books as I
marry them to silver and ribbon.

Vertigo isn't optional, or amathophobia.
I can ignore *Keep Off*
Ladder signs as I swing
Fred Astaire-like from the rungs.

At home, I doctor broken books,
bandage their torn skin.

My room grows shelves where,
outside their Eden, they multiply
like wild because that's what I'm given
for every holiday on the calendar.
I don't bother asking for anything else.

I date only bibliophiles—
my marriage bed is an inflatable
mattress on a box spring of books.

My spouse enters a book as a submarine,
can't hear me under all those words.

DEAR CHARLES

What was it like to have three wives?
It must have been confusing,
especially since you chose women with
rhyming names—Johannah, Susannah, and Hannah.

Did you call them all Anna?
Did you ever mix up their birthdays? children?
Was it like trying to read three books at once,
shelving and reshelving,

the plots entangling? I think it is nice
you married the first two
the same day,
to quell any first wife rivalry.

But when that November night wrapped you in her cold
arms,
which new wife lay in the next room,
alone? Day 1—the hierarchy
of heartache sets in.

Your brides were young: Johannah, nineteen;
Susannah, sixteen.
Seven years later, you added Hannah,
half your age.

Wasn't life hard enough
clearing trees, rocks, sage,
burning lime, and hauling timber?
Wasn't it hard enough to find food for one family?

Charles,
I hold two pictures of you:
one in your fine black mission suit, top hat,
cane, and Brigham Young beard;

another in your black and white prison stripes.
Four months in the pen outside Salt Lake City,
and here you are posing with apostles
smug as kings.

APPLES

1.

An apple is a womb.
A red house with a white room.
Eve comes calling.

2.

Statues of Thai dancers
on father's bookshelf, cheeks red
as apples, flex fingers backwards at impossible
angles. I thought them angels, imitated
those glitzy souvenirs from his
missionary years. He played guitar,
sang on stage about Jesus,
ate mangos where there were no apples.

3.

Sunday, and father slept alone,
curled in a womb
of white sheets. I found a knife,
tried to peel an apple for breakfast, the way they do on TV, one long curl.

4.

Blood deepened already red skin,
dappled white fruit. Sleeptorn
father
snatched blade, bandaged hand. I ate
blood and sweet.

5.

Summer, 1987,
I climbed the tree out back to gather apples,
still green. The tree grew ten, twenty, sixty feet.
An apple of hours,
core of fear,
blood on bark.
Finally, father. Home from work.
Reduced the tree to sixty, twenty, ten, and reached elongated
arms to swing me down. Green apples left to
redden, swell, left to windfall.

6.

I can't wrap my hands around this dolor—white
weight, skin smooth, cold core. Blood and sweet.

7.

After my own mission in Canada,
where I learned to eat blood of maples,
where I sang in subways with other missionaries
passing out scripture cards, free Bibles, trying to warm
in the crack of cold rejection, our black
clothes lined white with roadsalt,
shabby in tube light like a murder of shadows.

8.

Her eyes opened. Her blood
changed from immortal to corruptible.
She could connect the dots. When Eve ate,
it tasted like—
like bone meal,
angel cake,
bloodroot,
failing stars.

9.

Years later, I no longer believe. This I hand my father,
a green-to-red witness.

10.

When school's out, I take apples,
teach my daughters to slice straight down, even wedges
unpeeled, only heel of hand touches steel, fingers
backbent like Thai dancers.

11.

Eve's calling card.
The seed's sweet prison cell.
Gravity's doorbell.

POST-MORMONS ARE LEAVING

Post-Mormons are leaving the circled-up pioneer wagons
for wide open plains.

Post-Mormons are leaving crushed under ox-pulled wagon
wheels, their jaws broken, lungs punctured.

They bear heavy family trees on their shoulders, the weight
of generations, roots raking the earth.

They carry their children's children on their shoulders,
packs and handcarts filled with susurrate rust.

Post-Mormons are the new Ex-Mormons. Or rather, Post-
Mormons are Ex-Mormons who've swallowed embers and
live to say *That was me.*

Ex-Mormons see shards. Post-Mormons see a new bottle,
the old bottle standing by, other bottles near: glass flasks,
liquor cylinders, spirits bottles. Some tapered. Some ribbed.
Some squat and square.

Post, Latin for *after, behind*

Ex, Latin for *out of*

Post-Mormons, then, are the ticker tape *after* the parade,
fallen and trampled, swept together for recycling.

Ex-Mormons, then, are fugitives fleeing *out of*, refugees
from the bombed city, survivors of the kill zone, escapees.

Post-Mormons are leaving the harsh x (like hex) of the Ex-
Mormons and gathering their sorrow into the O of Post.

Post-Mormons are leaving the walled garden's satisfying fruit to scavenge glacial soil's mysterious sustenance.

They are leaving in droves, hemorrhaging from wards and stakes and missions around the world.

They aren't leaving because they want to get intimate with evil or because someone swapped their cream for 1 percent.

They're leaving because conscience needles. Because better angels prick. Because the path where they find their feet nettles, tricked with weeds.

They're leaving Bible bags. Missionary name tags. A stack of seminary manuals.

Post-Mormons hold an expired temple card. They remove their magic underwear, the magic gone, roll them and stack them like cords of white firewood, stow them in closets. Or shred them for cleaning cloths. Or burn them in a backyard bonfire.

Mine in a bedside bin. My husband's in the garage, boxed up.

Post-Mormons are teens in grownup bodies. They purple their hair. They ink their skin. They pierce noses and tongues and navels.

They are alcohol virgins. They hold a salt-rimmed margarita. A chilled sangria. A champagne flute.

They are coffee virgins. They drink their first latte. Order iced cappuccino. Sip mocha with whip.

They are smoke virgins. Some puff their first cigarette.
First cigar. First joint.

Their *Thou shalt nots* turn to *Why nots* or *Maybe nots*
or *I'd rather nots.*

Some leave husband or wife and kids. Attempt open
marriage. Come out.

My mother and her wife, married at the end of a long
December.

Post-Mormons walk barefoot over the wreckage of faith
crisis, exchange bleeding digits for free time. They take up
cycling and watercolor. They take up fly fishing and poetry.
They take up bartending and competitive Scrabble.

On Sunday, they hike or shop or sleep or clean house.

Sometimes they miss getting all dressed up and sitting
snug in a family pew and singing congregational hymns
and carols. The chapel's sanctuary a down quilt of quiet.

But those crazy angels with their hot pokers.

Post-Mormons are leaving in the night, trailing red
across a frozen river.

Post-Mormons are leaving, a quail flock following not
far behind.

Post-Mormons are leaving, a pocketful of sunflower seeds
to scatter as they go.

DEAR SUSANNAH

When the crickets descended on the crops like a curse,
you traded your mother's fine black silk dress from London
for a cow,
and harvested sego lily roots and sap from weeping willows.

Hannah, you write, was a "true and faithful" wife,
but you don't say much about Johannah, the Swede,
who barely spoke English, except she bore him nine
and you fourteen.

I think of how you were the first to bear
and lose. Two weeks alive,
one week in the grave,
and Johannah birthed a son.

He lived.
Your second died, too.
Johannah's lived.
A horrible arithmetic.

When she got her own house three miles from town,
in a low, boggy place,
she raised ducks and sons,
and walked to market every day—

a neat arrangement, the old homestead all yours
with plenty of space
for your chickens and children,
and the spirits of your dead daughters.

You had the smallest house, but Grandpa
lived with you most. As much as a man might try for
equity—in resources, in conjugal visits—
how can he ration affection?

Susannah,
in my nightmare, my husband's hand guides my hand
to stroke the pregnant belly
of my own Johannah.

My blood mother,
you stood at your husband's trial and refused to speak,
a stubborn witness,
content with your third.

PIONEER DAY

Freak show, a classmate said. Watch them parade
down Main on July 24th, singing *Come,*

Come Ye Saints, horse and wagon,
aproned women,
babies in gingham.

Toddlers in bonnets
on their fathers' shoulders,
men with tin cups lashed to belts.

A freak show she said, after a short
Utah residence. I told her

I'd marched in that parade,
sang loud *All Is well, All
Is well,* or sat curbside

on Logan's Center and 3rd
by the picturesque mansions
a polygamist built,

one for each of his three
families, ordinary
backdrop of my life, familiar as summer

sweat. I'd wave and clap
as the bishop rode by
with his pair of Clydesdales,

hooves heavy-clomping. He'd toss
a fistful of saltwater
taffy at my feet. I'd scramble

to gather each piece,
wrapped in a twist
of wax paper, as if

it were my right, my inheritance to grab
what I could from hot asphalt,
a pinch of scorch.

MISSIONARY WORK IN KANATA, CANADA

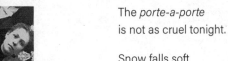

The *porte-a-porte*
is not as cruel tonight.

Snow falls soft
on a row of pastel houses,
where curves in the moulding,
louvered shutters,
and tidy lines of lights
make them look
like dollhouses.

Bibles in bags
slung over our shoulders,
we follow the unshoveled path
door   to door   to door.

Pink cloud cover
locks in heat
and hides an abyss
of black sky.
                    Under layers,
we are almost warm.

Door slams are muted
by snowfall masked as manna.

Tonight, nothing these dolls do
can hurt us.

PROSELYTIZING BY A MARIAN SHRINE IN QUÉBEC

Women walk *chemin du rosaire* in morning's
cold white dresses. Wrapped in our cloaks, we weather
snowy shoulders, withering stares. Take a card, *ma
dame*? In her eyes, were

years that gathered, ran down the well-worn grooves of
tears. *Est-ce que vous priez à elle?* We answer,
Non. She shakes the grief from her voice and welcomes
us to a service.

How can I, a traveler here, a woman,
ask these devotees to abandon Mary?
In my mind, a feminine goddess, throneless,
wanders. We enter.

Je vous salue, Marie pleine ... echoes through the
dim-lit nave. The arches, her fingers, bend and
hold. The windows pierce in between and make a
diadem. *Mère de*

Dieu, a wonder, hunger for softer gods is
spreading. Thousands blink at the endless prayers
spilled on lonely Father gods. Heaven's Mother,
where have we hidden?

Plant our souls with psalms for the Queen of Heaven.
Teach us dove song; lead us to lust for peacetime.
Wizen mouths. Enlarge our small hearts. Forgive us,
gentle us, Mother.

ELOHER

You caterpillar across the page
of our thoughts. Flight is imminent.
Wings are more than metaphor.
If Father is sun, and Son is moon,

You are salt on a black tablecloth.
You season everything, hurtle millions
of lightyears to be near
us. You are spores, snowflakes, particles

of yellow pollen. You are aspen saplings,
diamonds forged in darkness, grains of sand
under oyster tongues. You're neutrons,
You're sea foam, You're motes of dust

spinning in a shaft of afternoon light.
We're mammal, still look for you against our cheek.
We're marsupial, barely weaned from the pouch.
We're reptile, straining against the skin of our eggs

to reveal Your face.

MOTHER HAS A DEGREE IN EXTERIOR DESIGN

See how she offsets the Prussian blue of the bay
by its opposite on the color wheel,
the splendid burnt orange of a just-so sunset

And see how that lemon wedge of sun
draws the eye,
makes the colors pop

And over here—see how she's hung drops of dew
like a little string of holiday lights
on a spider's web

And see how the spider's pendulous body
droops like a gold earring
on the web's lobe

She's not afraid to use
every shade of green:
forest, shamrock, olive, jungle

She adores red:
hoodoos she hordes like knickknacks
in the cupboard of a Utah desert

Look up—see how she mixes and matches
edgy patterns of birds that verge on chaotic
with classic clouds and bolts of blue

And look how she arranges
all those migrants into Sanskrit
to make a prayer wheel of the sky

P-DAY AT THE SUGAR SHACK

This day brims with
too much sweetness.

The maple syrup, liquid gold,
we've poured into pea soup
and red Kool-Aid, over beans,
flapjacks, and sausage links.

We are the only patrons in this
cabane à sucre made to hold
a hundred. We crowd one table.
Our hosts watch curiously. Our voices
drift up, wraith-like, to the rafters.

Outside, troughs full of fallen snow
flank the sugar shack. We tip our
warm mugs of syrup over the snow
and twist popsicle sticks in the cooling
sugar to make maple suckers.

Our blood buzzes.
The woods of bare sugar maples
buzz with our laughter.

Buckets hang from the trees,
collecting. Others are connected
by thin purple tubes, reverse
IVs. After the sap is boiled down,
it will be served to the next guests.

Our vespertine shadows grow,
interlock with lengths of looming woods
and their woven shadows.
Our heavy boots press into the dark earth, wet
leaves, and dying snow.

The frozen ground is thawing,
turning to dark mud. The coldest
winter of our lives is unlocking.

GODS' HARVEST DANCE

From cloud cloth she cuts a fabric fine and tinseled,
edges soaked in wine and white middled. Needled
pine she pins to pattern, runs through with silver river
threaded line. When done, a full skirt she sets on
mountain mannequin till Michaelmas and the harvest
dance. Then watch her spin and spin across the sky.
Rivers flash like lightning. Her bare feet smashing
as she heel-toe-heel-toes it across a field of rye.
Father's there stomp-clapping, keeping time.
They hook elbows, dancing Drops of Brandy, book it
right over the county line, His and Hers, yours and mine.

RING TRICKS

> And again, verily I say unto you, if a man marry a wife
> by my word, which is my law, and by the new and
> everlasting covenant . . . [the marriage] shall *be of full force*
> *when they are out of the world.*
> —an excerpt from Doctrine and Covenants 132:19

> *I gave my love a ring and made him swear*
> *Never to part with it;*
> —Portia, *The Merchant of Venice*

O, the whelps we were then. Mooncalves.
Greenhorns. When we traded rings,

we believed the secret inscription
we'd had engraved on their inner skins,

God's promise to the elect: marriage that would stretch
to infinity, defying death.

We believed if good enough,
we'd have each other. Always.

Now when we think of that scripture,
we see the shadow it casts

beneath its glimmershow of promise—
Joseph Smith said he asked God

why the old prophets could marry
more than one wife. God's answer: righteous

posterity. God's command:
bring the practice back to raise up

children in the new faith, the eternal
covenant. When Joseph wrote down

this revelation and showed his first,
Emma, she combusted

the paper, thrust it in the hearthfire,
not wanting to share her Joseph,

her husband. And while mainstream Mormons
now shun plural marriage,

a man can still be eternally sealed
to more than one wife in a serial

progression, but the same is not true
for women. They have one shot at queendom.

When I married you, I didn't think
hard about heaven's polygamous

threat, sheep-clothed in church doctrine,
but let's face it—I've never been good

at sharing, even trifling things
like chocolate, or my pillow, or my floss.

We exchanged rings, swore oaths, made the secret
-sacred clasp with our virginal hands.

We couldn't foresee, thirteen years later,
our rings would end up on the fingers of

diametrically different people,
who take honey with vinegar,

luminance with shade, our orthodoxy
changed, etched over, effaced

by our palimpsestuous selves.

I COULD NEVER BE A JEHOVAH'S WITNESS

I mean no offense to J-dubs,
but I like celebrations too much

to give them up. I love the smell
of the pumpkin I gut
with my girls,

the plink of the seeds in the bowl
of viscera, Jack's crooked grin lit
by a candle. I love

the pause in the rush of life
for a day of Grace,
the long table laden,

and the bowl of olives I place
by my plate. They are Russian fur caps
on my fingertips. I love

the lace doilies and pizzas
shaped as hearts, the chalky taste
of our conversation. Holidays, I

sprinkle the tabletop with flour
and guide the cookie cutters
to the edges. Circles would not be

the same. I would miss birthdays,
ache to whip up the cakes
my kids pick out, like strawberry

with blue frosting and candy pearls.
Those pearls I won't give up,
not even for God. And anyway,

my made-to-order deities
would be the smiling kind,
the rolling laughter,

the squeal and clap after candles
blow themselves out,
cheering for our little light.

MOSES REMOVED HIS SHOES

You slip off your sandals
to enter the quiet sanctuary   of the room
where our children sleep
bend down to hear their breath
rearrange the crazy angles   of their limbs
blanket them   again
sweeping sweaty hair from their faces

You rest your hand   on the doorframe
slip on your sandals
wearing only   night garments
the ones with holes
in the right sleeve
and the left thigh
and a look of thoughtfulness

You perform this ritual
each night before bed   It must be
your prayer   you who have not prayed in so long
entrance   into the holy of holies
your bush ablaze on Mount Sinai
Their small faces
glow   envelope you in their wake

PON FARR

In the absence of Vulcan mind melds
and Betazoid empathic powers,
we fall back on human abilities to read
each other, our imperfect
transference of inflected syllable
and raised eyebrow, our faulty
system of sentences, gestures.

Would we be better off
Borg? All hive mind, hooked up
to the neural paths of each others'
thoughts, emptying into and drawing
from the same deep reserve.
No guesswork. In sync. But our tech doesn't extend
that far. My laconic love, I want to touch

your logical face, thumb in the dip
between chin and lip, fingers bracing
cheek bone's arch. I want
to close my eyes and exit nerve's blue shoots,
channeling through your Jeffries tubes,
turbolifts, warp engine. What's hiding
here, on the holodeck? A banquet hall

with table runners, roasted swan,
fistfuls of rose petals? Tarnished candelabras
lighting up a boar's head on the wall?
I want the old blood fever to take, blaze
the cold grate, so even across the room,
we can sense each other's
temperatures rise—you in dress uniform,

or no uniform at all.

THIRTY-THREE REASONS WHY: A PARTIAL LIST

Because the glazed strawberries at the restaurant are red hearts, waiting.

Because an hour later, beneath a brazen angel's gaze, we immortals sit on temple hill to survey a valley of promise.

Because on the sticky vinyl of the backseat, your electric pinkie skims mine.

Tongues, you teach me, are soft and warm, nights dizzy with stars.

When I serve you an accidental hairball on your spaghetti, you don't run for the door.

When I serve you a volleyball, you know how to pepper— bump, set, hit.

And when we kneel at the altar, you play an allegro beat on the drum of my heart.

Because our first night together, two icebergs learn to melt.

And when we move far from the warmth of family, you are a furnace against loneliness.

Because your legs look chiseled in slick blue running shorts, Michelangelo out for a jog.

Possibly, it's the pout of your face when you read, the pucker of your brows when I spend too much, the slack of your jaw when I show you the little white stick, the parallel pink lines.

Because you pull over and don't look away when my stomach rebels. By the gas station. By the river. In the tall grass near the church parking lot.

It's our daughters' chins.

And your dark brown turning to cinnamon in their eyes.

It's Sunday afternoon when you, the new Piper of Hamlin, sway them with your music.

It has something to do with the way your resting hand makes a T in sign language.

It has everything to do with your whispered *mi amor* and my answer, *mon amour*.

Because the lure of the universe pulls you out on a cool night in March to witness the geometry of the moon holding hands with two planets and quietly singing.

Because you are a mountain boy with rivers in your veins.

And you turn over river rocks to show our girls the Mayflies.

And press their eyes to binoculars to see a glacier's blue ice.

Because you revive fish after the catch, deliver them to the wet grace of second life.

Sometimes you come home early smelling like Old Spice and massage the place where wings grow.

It has a little to do with the sounds you make when you
sleep and the way your knees make a tent of our sheets, as
familiar now as a ticking clock, as the taste of salt.

It has a little to do with the oxytocin your sleeping form
settles on me like a humidifier's mist.

And when the cat of my sadness leaps onto your lap
casually during dinner, you let it sit there, feeling the bones
of its shoulder blades with your thumbs.

And on Sunday nights our scriptures are heavy tomes of
Shakespeare pillowed by our thighs, our open palms.

It's the brown and red and silver in your beard.

It's the cello of your voice, the vibration of your chest
against the audience of my ear.

It's slow sex at midnight in soft, half-asleep dreaminess.

Because I hate to share and because you don't believe
in polygamy.

Because both of us are part rose, part thorn.

And because breath is better from your mouth, still warm.

WHEN I BEACH

> *A relationship with God is the best*
> *relationship you can have.*
> — Facebook meme

I'll say this—God doesn't have your hands,
your broad shoulders, your way of breathing.

He's never stroked my skin from thigh
to floating rib, or kissed my forehead,
the gate of my lips, the prayer book of my palm.

I can sleep without God right at my side,
but when you're gone for a night I'm
swallowed like Jonah in the fish's dark stomach.

It's your face I pray to see when I beach
on the sunlit shore of morning,
my legs tangled in a froth of white sheets,

your smile drawing me up
through a surf of bleak dreams.

FORMER MORMONS CATECHIZE THEIR KIDS

In the beginning was—

    Chaos. Cyclone. Sky.

In the beginning was—

    Death. Hunger. The Void.

    A thought. A Word. Matter unorganized.

    A Big Bang. An expanding universe.
    Heavy elements formed in supernovan heat.

    A lotus on a lake of milk. A mass of water
    humming Nun. Fire of Muspell and ice of Niflheim
    and emptiness of Ginnungagap.

    A baobab tree. An egg-shaped cloud.
    Sea slime emergent land.

    A white-blossomed tree that gives corn and light.
    A black-and-white deer.

In the beginning was—

    The Creator, who made his nephew Sotuknang.
    Rangi and Papa, Heaven and Earth. Olorun,
    neither male nor female, transcending both.

    There was Gaia, Mother Earth; Eros, desire;
    and Tartarus, the Underworld.

    There was Brahma, splitting self into matching selves,
    like cell mitosis, in order to mate himself to herself.

There was Ymir the frost giant sweating children
from his armpits.

The Spirit Master of the Center of Heaven,
The August Wondrously Producing Spirit, and
The Divine Wondrously Producing Ancestor.

There was the Spirit World, Heavenly Mother and Father,
and their billions of spirit children. Elohim, the powerful ones.
Mashé Manido, the Great Spirit.
The Kingdom of Everlasting Truth
ruled by the Naba Zid-Wendé.

A pantheon of gods—

Sa, God of Death, and his eloper son-in-law,
Alantangana. Buri, licked free from an ice block
by the good cow Audhumla. Izanagi and Izanami,
descended from the Floating Bridge of Heaven
to birth Japan's islands.

The Hero twins, Xbalanque and Hunahpu, ballplayers
and bird demon slayers. There was Manabush,
the Great Rabbit, thieving tobacco and first fire
for his people. The giant Pan Gu, whose voice was thunder
and whose breath was wind.

Jesus, unscrolling the skin of his chest to reveal
his sacred heart, sword-skewered and aflame.
Obatala with his snail shell of sand and long golden
chain and sacred egg near his heart.

There was Odin Allfather, Thor, thunder god,
and Loki, trickster, who turned mare and bore
the eight-legged colt Sleipnir.

A pantheon of goddesses—

With her lioness head, Tefnut, goddess of moisture,
greening the Nile River valley. Aset of the cow horns
and golden disk. Hut Heru, goddess of delights
rattling her sistrum. Nebet Hut, goddess of service,
in her hands a mummy's linen.

Spider Woman, spinner of Life. Tiamat, goddess
of salt seas, whose tear tracks are the Tigris
and Euphrates. Nü Wa, the lonely goddess, who melted
river rocks to patch the breaking sky.
Bright-Shining-Woman, who says when a baby
will come or when a woman will bleed.

Athena, grey-eyed goddess of wisdom, bursting
from her father's frontal lobe fully armored.
Aphrodite, born of her castrated father's spilled seed
in a frothy foam of fecundity. Demeter with her
wheat sheaf. Artemis with her silver arrows
and bow. Hera of the peacock.

Skadi on her frozen skis. The Valkyries whisking
the wounded away, bearing the battle-fallen
to Valhalla. Frigg the foreknowing. Hel,
daughter of Loki, gathering in the sickened
and elderly. Freya and her falcon-feather cloak.
Idunn and her juvenescent apples.

And they made humans—

> They made them from spittle mixed with yellow,
> red, white, and black earth. They made them from
> driftwood they found on shore. They sprang whole
> from Ra's tears.

> They transformed them from bear, eagle, beaver,
> sturgeon, wolf, and crane. They made them from
> turquoise, Mexican opal, red ochre, white clay,
> abalone, pollen, iron ore, white rock, jet, and water
> scum. From the blood of slain enemy gods
> they made them.

> They made them black, a strong color, different
> from the red sun and the white moon.
> The Earthmaker baked them in a hearth: half-baked
> white, overbaked black, and just-right red.
> Moon made love to Eveningstar, and on the third day
> girls and boys were born.

And the humans were named—

> Eve and Adam. Selu and Kanáti. Ancestral Woman
> and Ancestral Man.

> La'ila'i and Ki'i and Kane. Pyrrha and Deucalion.

And the purpose of humans?

> They were shaped to be slaves, to free lesser gods
> from labor. They were made to assuage the ache
> of loneliness. They were made in the image of Elohim,
> male and female.

They were made by accident, spilled to earth in Ra's
sorrow. They were made like little clay pets,
baked or breathed on to give them life. They were made
to be tried and tested. Would they obey their gods?

They were made to worship and remember
their creator.

And did they remember?

On the made world, they forgot the creator
again and again.

Yaweh greened a garden paradise called Eden,
and the humans were expelled for eating forbidden fruit.
The gods regretted their human creations.
Earth was purged.

Some people were saved by burrowing down to live
with ants, sharing their food, the ants tightening
and tightening their tiny belts.

Some humans were saved in an ark, a floating zoo,
while the creator erased the slate. First by fire,
then ice, then flood. Glaciers melted, ice caps
shrank, polar bears went hungry. A great flood.

And that multihue ribbon arcing across the blue?

God's promise he's done with the flooding.
And the elite path to Midgaard.
And our sun prismed by airborne droplets.

And the future of humankind and the earth?

>The four horsemen of the apocalypse will bring death,
>famine, war, and conquest. Christ will come again
>in robes of red. Gog and Magog will drink all the water
>of Tiberius.

>The great wolf Fenrir will swallow the sun
>and Yggdrasil the world tree will burn. Sa, God of Death,
>will come to claim Alantangana's descendants.
>Fire and ice. Flood and desolation.

>The world will grow hotter and hotter, like a giant
>greenhouse smothered in sunheat, unless—

Wherein lies redemption?

>In the prophets who spin stories for their people:
>Abraham and his seed numerous as stars;
>Moses with his brazen serpents on a staff;
>Jesus guiding the doubter's hand to his perpetual
>wounds; Mohammed dictating the Angel Gabriel's
>words; Buddha meditating in a lotus; Elijah's empty
>chair; Joseph Smith peering into a dark hat at the
>peep stone, words floating up to his eyes in
>phosphorescing light.

Wherein lies redemption?

>In the prophetesses who lead: Miriam helping to
>guide her people through the desert; Deborah
>deliberating under a date tree; Anna pronouncing
>the child good. Eliza R. Snow penning poems about

Heavenly Mother. Emily Dickinson sewing her
fascicles by candlelight. Mother Teresa lifting scraps
of bodies from the streets. Jane Goodall learning the
language of chimpanzees. Malala in sunset headscarf
telling her story on stage.

Wherein lies redemption?

In parents turning their hearts to their children,
children turning their hearts to their parents.

In shorter showers and flicking off the unused lamp,
hybrid buses and solar power.

In sharing poems, songs, stories by lovelight,
this web of wondrous narratives.

DEAR SUSANNAH

When my own Charles leaves
(for Texas or Madrid),
I watch the TV shows he can't abide,
introduce the girls to childhood
faves that landscape my personal mythologies—

David Bowie as the Goblin King,
Atreyu hunting the purple buffalo,
Princess Buttercup in the fire swamp. We indulge
in pizza, popcorn, fudge, a holiday
built around the nucleus of his absence.

Did you burn the midnight oil pouring over scripture,
perhaps the passage in Genesis
where Sarah humbles Hagar,
or did you shuffle pearwood bobbins,
tatting some new pattern of grace?

Did you ever relish those solitary hours,
when he was with your sisterwives,
Hannah and Johannah? Or was it always a millstone
of ache? After I tuck the girls in, I sleep light
when he's gone, even with neighbors,

cell phones, deadbolts, 911. I quake
at a dog's bark, curse
birds scuffling in the leaves, and the rough

roof-scamper of squirrels.
With your eight children bedded for the night,

your homestead in grizzly territory,
with Native neighbors on land you stole,
settling without permission, I imagine
you didn't sleep at all. Or perhaps you slept
curled up to the cold

barrel of whatever gun he could spare.

FOUNDER'S DAY

was this holiday Grandma hated,
not because men dressed up as Indians,
but because they smelled boozy

when they rode in to torch
a playhouse-sized cabin.
She must've inherited her disdain

from the cluck of her mother's tongue. Still,
Grandma gathered with neighbors to commemorate
the founding of their town, as if

it'd been hidden, as if the Western Shoshone
hadn't lived, hunted, fished in Cache Valley
for generations. Cache for the pelts

mountain men stashed there, Cache
from French *cacher*, to hide. I want to hide
my ignorance in a mountainside cave,

pile snow on top of a clever door. I've never met
any of the children
adopted by my parents' parents, dark step

-siblings at the family photo's edge.
Did Grandma tell her adoptive children
about Founder's Day, label it

Heritage or Tradition, how onlookers cheered
when soldier-pioneers drove the Indians off
with cap guns in a battle

sham. But *"was* this holiday" is wrong, I learn,
when I search and find footage
from last September.

Revise the past tense. They
dress up. They ride
in. They torch.

Black wigs and feathered headdresses,
men smeared red from waist to neck.
Another pack in plaid shirts trigger

fake rifles. And casually strewn
on blankets or bleachers, drinking
cola or Kool-Aid, holding children high,

onlookers cheer.

REVISION

It's at least 200 years overdue,
what was needed in this place—
a good earthquake.

It slips from your mouth, Mom,
hits, finally, in the clothing store,
one seismic word—

bisexual.

We step outside.
Mountains spin.
The word *sin*

chokes in my throat,
acid bleak
I swallow back.

A ten-year secret,
a whole decade to revise,
to re-see with new eyes.

You say you were afraid
to let me down again.
You were right then—

thirty years of Sunday lessons learned,
rules for heaven, hell,
made me a person you couldn't tell.

Around us now
lie whole mountains
made low.

Leveled,
I offer a nude
I don't know.

DEAR MOM

December lady, the day you came out to me I was in my
hibernacle, so comfortable in the warm smell of my own
pelt and the cave's dry envelope where I slept in a ball,

dreaming of silver fish and spring. You startled me awake
with your crunching feet, bearing news through a fresh fall.
I had smelled winter from my hideaway, but you took me

by the paw. Accustomed to dark, my eyes sought blindly—

/ Snow sheathed the pine needles. /

You showed me what I'd slept through at every hint of frost.

/ Snow sculpted into waves. /

No doubt, you feared the probability of my bite, my claws.

/ Snow fell soft, each flake filigreed, scintillant. /

You're human, after all, and one swipe could've finished you.
I took off my thick coat, felt cold's blow, what you'd borne these
hush-mouth years. I yanked teeth from my jaws—how sharp—

tore razors from my fingers—how many cuts—left den behind.
Shoulder to shoulder in my ample fur, you teach me to forage
for winterberry and root—no need to devour your heart.

VESTIGIAL

> *Lost belief, like a lost fortune, has effects that linger.*
> —Jack Miles, *God: A Biography*

I catch my husband on the couch
cheating,

        reading scripture, St. Luke,
        Christ hunched under his cross

on the via dolorosa.
Thirty-three

        when we walked out of church
        for the last time,

after a sermon on how persecuted
we Mormons are. This

        after California's Prop 8. After SCOTUS
        gave a thumbs up on gay marriage

and LDS leaders refused
to renege.

        The backyard tree's white blossoms
        molt, shed pristine

petals for spring's greenery.
Easter, and this church

itch. Thirty-three, the same age as Christ
crucified, we decided on a respite

from the religion we'd metabolized
since babyhood, we'd preached to foreigners, we'd

taught our children. But though we've shed
our first unfurling, our roots

remain. I will always obey
traffic lights, teachers' instructions, and rules

for the Oxford comma. I will exorcise
orthodoxy waving grand *Fuck Yous* at cross-

walks, alarm clocks, and death's heavy
finality. *I think there was something between*

Christ and John, says my husband, done
with his reading. John the Beloved.

Christ bleeding and broken, cruciate,
pointing to his lover: *Mother, behold thy son.*

OUR LORD JESUS IN DRAG

This guy can walk on anything,
even six-inch stilettos.
His purse, a sequined fish,
he unzips to finger a two-drachma coin,
flings it at the sour faces
of the unbelieving bouncers.

He doesn't need Spanx, perfect
abs, perfect butt, perfect legs stretch
from the glittering hem
of his little black dress
stitched with stars.

He struts the floor to the backroom
where his twelve gussied-up friends
fondle him in welcome. They gab
while they sample the grub, get
a little drunk, tongues down throats
that taste like red wine.

Later, they'll hit the town,
paint it rainbow, raise the dead, raise
hell, before Jesus goes home, strips,
scrubs make-up from his perfect face.

In the morning, it'll be a dove grey
suit, cufflinks, a power tie.
All business, he'll forgive
a hundred stinging slights,
his daily sponge of vinegar.

THE MERCY OF MUD

Mom, tell me again about the time
Grandpa backed up the car
on his way to work, barely paused

when he felt the rear left tire
go bump
before he heard Grandma's

scream
trapped behind window glass and your
wail. Tell me

again of the mercy
of mud, how you had
toddled to the car, to your dad, then

fell, how the
melon of your
skull sank

into rain-
softened earth as
rubber drove your head

down. How he ran to snatch
welter of shock,
wipe muck from feather

hair, cradle whimper and wrack.
Tell me how
after, you were never the same,

how those we love
crush
our most vulnerable

parts, press them to
terror,
how some wounds

are too intricate to heal.

THE DISPOSAL OF MORMON GARMENTS

This ritual, for me, used to entail careful cutting, excising the horizontal line over knee and navel, the compass's V over the left breast, the square's L over the right, four white rounds of cloth with their holy symbols I'd hold between tweezers and carefully burn over the sink, rinsing down cinders and wiping away scorch marks on porcelain.

Their sacred bits stripped, I ripped the remaining cloth to rags, perfect for soaking up lemon oil polish on the piano and bookshelves.

V   E   I   L

I remember putting them on the first time—I was 21, prepping for a mission to Montreal. All missionaries go through the temple before they're sent to distant lands, armored, so to speak, in garments. In a dressing room of the Logan Temple, after the washing and anointing ordinance, I pulled on the bottoms, slipped the top over my head. I chose dry silk fabric, felt its soft caress beneath my dress on chest and legs. I loved its cool, soft touch, like a slip sewn into my clothes, whisper on skin. It felt secret and sexy, yet virtuous, good. I embraced my newly bizarre faith, what I'd seen in the temple wholly alien. The clothes, the prayers, the hand gestures. Tokens and signs and shields. Garments were easy compared to the rest. The rest clung like sunburn.

V   E   —   L

I remember removing them for the last time. I'd taken a sabbatical from church attendance, and the months stretched, unraveling any desire I had to return.

Why am I still wearing these? I asked myself.

A 12 years' habit, I answered.

I didn't have any other underwear, had to go to the store—*What is my size?*—to buy a package—*Should I choose white? Hipsters or briefs? What fabric do I like? Spandex? Cotton?* After an hour of painful deliberation, a package in pastels—not white, but not a loud red or black or striped. No lace or frills. Cotton Hanes for Her. Size 7, I guessed, not bikini cut or square, but not spinsterly, either. So many, too many choices emanating from one.

        V   —   —   L

For months, I felt naked under my clothes, wore a tank top under my blouse, leggings beneath my jeans. When I'd forget to don a camisole, I felt exposed, cold, too much air on my midriff instead of a garment top's insulating hug. I realized some of my shirts were semi-transparent, which hadn't mattered with garments. They'd lent a layer of substance to any shirt. Rather than downsizing my wardrobe, I bought undershirts in every conceivable color.

        V   —   —   —

I remember the stories I heard in church—bullets deflected, burns absorbed—by the power of garments worn by faithful members. But for me, faithless, they've lost all magic. The care, ritual, mysticism, respect I've shed. I empty the bin beside my bed, bag the dry silk, maternity tops, cotton bottoms cleaned and packed here four years ago in case ...

They smell of must. I slip them in a plastic garbage sack like the carcasses of doves, all feather and rot, bodies devoid of spark. I toss them in the dumpster's dark.

DEAR MAY

> *You choose your ancestors.*
> —Ralph Ellison

You lie in Logan, our hometown, buried
not far from my grandpa, the one with pincers
and a fireman's ashy badges. And not far from a high
school friend with a gap-toothed smile she hid
behind her hand, stabbed in a parking lot when she was nineteen.

Let me start again. Dear May Swenson, I'm afraid to go
where you've gone, so I'm trying to rake my heart
into a Zen garden. Is it true you had to remove your name
from your mailbox so the Mormon missionaries
would leave you alone? They leave me

alone. Just one letter a month from a woman
I've never met. She writes, "Any effort made for
the happiness of others lifts us above ourselves,"
which means she believes her letters are stuffed
with blue morphos and honeycomb.

Sister—can I call you that?—I wonder if it was hard for you
as it was for me, a vivisection of lungs, each lobe shot
virus blue. The eldest of ten children,
you quickened into queerness like a spring bud's mad
unravel. Me the middle child of eight, learning my mother's love's

gender-blind, spanning oceans and continents
I'd narrowly imagined. You left Mormonism behind like an old world
mirror where you saw yourself darkly. I was thirty-three when I left,
denuded, strange as the alien shape of a newborn's head, its cord
-strangled lips half a gasp. You said the poet needs

no religion, that poetry and spirituality are redundant.
You rebaptized yourself with language, reconfirmed a tongue
of fire settling Pentecostal on your word-wilding art. Yours is the
legacy I would name myself to, would willingly inherit. Yours
the prayer I would pray, an orison of sound and sense and shape.

DEAR ELLEN, 2018

I used to think it old-fashioned, fuddy duddy,
didn't relish telling school buddies what a dusty
volume I tucked between the bookends
of my names, what funny shape was at the core
of my fruit if you sliced straight through.
Not a star, but this *Ellen*.

Then I opened Heaney's *Beowulf* in grad school
and saw the Old English raw on the page, *ellen*,
which the poet translates as *heroic*.

Hero who left a brutish husband and Manchester's
familiar for a new country's blank. Brave lady
who forsook your foremother's faith for a new truth,
one that sang to you out of the dark.
I know it's the hardest

trek I've taken. Ellen,

despite shards in the pane, we climb through.

STUDY FOR BELIEF WITH LINES
FROM *STAR TREK: THE ORIGINAL SERIES*

?) Let every sentence begin: I have been grossly mistaken.

The stars are gone. Kirk: *Kindly tell me what happened to the stars.*

Kierkegaard shuttles past Reason to planet Absurd, a gas giant

without a detectable landing pad. He says, it's the leap that matters.

We're being pulled toward the center of the zone of darkness.

Kenosis required, emptying the self of self. His sky lit, mine blazes

black, an experimental physics. Doubt the gravity that repels, attracts.

Dark energy : Dark matter : Attempt to probe : Universe [Static].

Neil deGrasse Tyson: *we are a speck on a speck on a speck*

on a speck. Spock: *Call it deep understanding.*

I'm trying to compensate for loss *Red Alert. [High-pitched tone]*

of life support of coordinates of light of lift. *The heart of the wise*

inclines to the right, but the heart of the fool to the left. Adrift

at a dextral spiral's galactic edge, her loosely-wound arms

unwinding, her central bulge a black hole's

guess. I divorce myself from fearmongers and god metaphors,

yet—

Apollo-alien, begging for adoration as he smites, smiles.

Child-alien, booming behind a blue face, all thunder-threat.

Amoeba-alien, sucking up starshine like an enormous vacuum.

'Twas grace that taught my heart to fear and grace my fears relieved.

Can this ship retract from a space hole, one that eats thrust?

I could write: 'Twas love that taught my mind to doubt, and love my doubts

increased. *As we draw closer to the source, it grows stronger.*

We grow weaker. We don't know what we don't know—

a critical failure. *Call it deep understanding.* I can't course

correct after complete engine meltdown, fuel spent, clinging to cargo.

Zone of darkness or—? *I'm getting telemetry* on the bridge

pushing buttons, turning knobs, neon flash and whir,

wired to what? *Shields up.* Stage set or power source? I'm ionized negative,

charged with tiny circles bearing minus signs. *What was it you sensed?*

A touch of death. Feel haptic down halls, fuzzed in brain fog. *How can I grant*

what I don't understand? Is it sinistral, this left-leaning, this waywardness?

And he shall set the sheep on his right hand, but the goats on the left.

Transporters and communication systems—offline.

My warp core drained clear. How to bring back its blue pulse?

Or is it better, translucent? Ladder rungs removed. Stairs—

What was it you sensed? Astonishment—phaser-blasted.

Jammed turbolifts. Sealed conduits. Is up a place (I want to be

VOLVELLE

96

Made from circles of paper or parchment,
the volvelle was part timepiece, part floppy disk,
and part crystal ball.
—Rheagan Martin, *The Getty Iris*

More than the bishop's gold crosier
with a face hidden somewhere in the wooden staff;
more than the sketches made from early

microscopes of bugs' wings interlaced;
more than the illuminated Christ on his cross
with drawback curtain of red grenadine;

Here in the Folger Shakespeare Library,
among the display of sixteenth-century books,
this one snags my roving attention—

I hunch over the volvelle.
From Latin *volvere*—to turn, I turn and turn
the volvelle in my mind like a sin

of omission. Two rundells revolve on a paper pivot,
arms that could point the path of the *solis*
and *luna*, or could determine

a Universal Address by aligning starlight.
Nine letters representing the nine names of God
swivel into sacred combinations,

an invention meant to settle all
religious disputes, though I'm not sure how
arranging nine names could quell

any differences, calm any heads.
I admit I believed brads and paper wheels
the make-do of kindergarten teachers

conjuring small magic to captivate
their captors, spin a few minutes
into a few hours. Hard to believe

these little devices, paper astrolabes,
were once labeled dark arts, shunned
by skeptics, resentful of their sussurate

prophecies. A cautious sort myself, I confess
I whisper past glass, *Prophesy*
to me, unwind, unfold, say which

is which. Then I hold my breath,
watch for the twitch.

WITH GRANDMOTHER-IN-LAW,
MUSEUM OF FLORIDA HISTORY

I have to pull her underwear down
three times. She half sits, half stands by the toilet,
the stall door ajar to fit us both.
I met her at a wedding eight years ago,
barely conversed between bites of cake.

She doesn't know that she doesn't know me.
Give her a ball of tissue, remind her to wipe.
Will she remember how?
She does. My relief is a mountain.
Squirt soap on her sore-pocked hands,

offer a paper towel the texture of her skin,
lead her by the arm to a heavy door
hung with a full-length mirror.
I think I know her, she says. *It's been a long
while, though.* In the waiting area, deliver her

like a tray of torn bread, *body of Christ,*
to her spouse, and continue the tour, their feet
shuffling behind—Mastodon bones,
taxidermy birds, blind eyes on me, and phantoms
in military uniform, trapped in glass.

WE CHRISTEN THE CANOE *SUNDAY SCHOOL*

For silver lake, and mist scudding water,
knocking boats at the dock, and oarlocks,
plastic ponchos made from garbage sacks,
and the hour of rain that made us miserable, thank you.

Thank you for a warm wind luffing us dry,
and blue minnows of smoke rising between pines,
a rope of cloud settled across the green,
its white partition bisecting mountains.

For the rut of college kids on the beach,
their aluminum canoes roped for tug-of-war,
the six packs of boys, thin bikinis of girls,
their laughter rioting across the water, thank you.

Thank you for the visitation of an osprey,
dipping deeply over silver surface,
for her choppy, lop-sided ascent,
spark of scales, tailfin in her talons.

For a rainbow caught on a dry fly,
the rich gold of its coin eyes,
copper flecks in pectoral fins,
silver glimmer of its belly, thank you.

Thank you for a careful knife inserted in the fish's anus,
for a silent score to accompany the gutting,
these daughters who satellite their father,
hands over mouths as fish viscera drift off. Thank you.

Thank you for teeming canoes and kayaks splashing,
a flotilla of paddleboats churning,
a motorboat's steady whine and white wake,
and a beatific quiet after its passing.

STAINED GLASS

You can't be afraid of cuts, the glazier says,
showing her hands
beautiful with scars.

She works with gloves on,
protected from slivers hidden
in the wood table's grain.

But on occasion, she sweeps her hand
over the table's surface
and snags the fabric of her skin.

A hazard of the profession,
a few cells in exchange
for the privilege of dying light

different colors—the blue folds
of Mary's robe, the red of Jesus' blood,
the milk of his skin

when he's pulled
from the brown cross, the green
stems of lilies announcing: Life.

All these hues paint your face
the colors of reverence,
whether you believe or not,

as you sit or kneel in church, any
church. Perhaps an old abbey with tall
columns, hunky punks, a rose window,

and sunlight
genuflecting through clouds
to worship at the altar of her art.

WHALE WATCHING

The morning's fog is thick as frosted glass.
Every wave's shadow and sea-drifting log
breathes innuendo. Strain eyes to their limits, ears
perched alert for the spurt of water to signal

their surfacing. A pod of females follows her
through the Salish Sea, hunting for Chinook salmon.
Walk the half-mile trail south to north, north
to south, south to north. Commandeer a picnic bench

and wait, unpack sandwiches, stare at water,
and don't dare let your eyes wander.
Hike up to the lighthouse and wait.
Hike down to the old kiln and wait.

Seals. Moss. Purple starfish big as backpacks.
Pull out binoculars. Cameras. And wait.
Watch for her girls club, imagine her sleek
dorsal fin higher than our heads, her black back

like a moving hill, weaving in and out of water,
sewing big stitches in the dark blue bay.
She's circling round these islands
where we live our little lives.

Her massive grace. Her godsome body.

IF MOTHER BRAIDS A WATERFALL

in a country where no one speaks
Her language   if She's a shrine
few bow to, few supplicate   if She's a book

no one reads, verses
rich as incantation   if Mother weaves a forest
floor from tree roots in a swath of clear

cut   if She untangles rivers into tributary
threads, the beds long since dry   if
She's a gold rush with no prospectors, a queen

bee with no drones, honeycomb
without attendants   if in the morning, Mother conducts
a chorus of larks   if at night, a throng of nightingales

if Her children sleep through the song   if She holds a rope
through an oubliette's trapdoor, calls
down to us, but we focus on the guard

pushing grub through the bean slot
once a day, *his* thrilling fingertips, *his* footstep echoing
as he walks away   if we look up at last   if we relearn Mother

Tongue through hard listening   if She's the One and Only, not
one of many   a claire-voie of Egyptian glass
in the stucco's arabesque   a gold seam for our broken

-ness, our shards   an arroyo parched for the rain
of our praise   if She's
starscape, all dark and blaze and hungry for our eyes

STILL MORMON

1.

I'm Mormon the way stars—rubbed out at noon,
robbed by sun—still burn

2.

The way a geode empty of its quartz
is still stone

3.

The way a whisper is still a breath
carved by tongue and teeth

4.

I'm Mormon the way a cathedral is still a cathedral, even after
iconoclasts shatter the windows, decapitate the saints,

5.

blunt their hands, topple their trunks from tiered niches,
tear them from cubbies, pillars, plinths,
a restoration of plain glass letting in
bolts of austere grey silk-light

6.

I'm Mormon the way a Greek Orthodox is primarily Greek
and less orthodox,
my own icons gathered under sky-blue domes—

7.

Madonna of Sagebrush, her foot crushing crickets,
seagull perched on her shoulder,
Liahona in her left hand, sego lily in her right,
beneath her image a red desert
where all may light a beeswax candle to illuminate her
honied look, beneficent smile

8.

The way you can take the girl out of Utah but can't take Utah
out of the girl, the way my hair and skin settle into dry
heat and Cache Valley smog, my shoulders Wellsville peaks,
my paunch and thighs Wasatch foothills, my veins mapping
Bear River on right and Logan River on left, all their tributaries,

9.

lakes, marshes, canals, brooks, streams, ditches, rills

10.

I'm Mormon the way a swimmer caught in riptide and carried out
makes peace with blue death but wears a thin suit
of hope that her body will be transmuted into

11.

something lovely and holy: sea star, anemone, tiger shark,
more than watermark left to fade on the page, more than a name
writ in water

12.

I'm Mormon the way the deeply drowned tree
ghosting beneath the boat is still tree

13.

The way a sugar maple tapped of its sweetness
stretches its leaves to hold the sun

14.

How the choir keeps singing after the beautiful
organ fails, wind moving through brass pipes
not making a sound, and the singers robed in velvet
continue acapella,
emerald voices floating luminous like curls of prayer-smoke

15.

How the valley dweller watches her mountains glow,
giants jeweled on a wildfire night, how she grows as close as she dares
to damage, to catastrophe, wills the chopper pilot safe journey
from lake to lick of flame

16.

How the valley dweller remembers the green hill
hid in an April shroud

17.

Like the peahen in the empresses' menagerie
among the glossy, iridescent eyes

18.

Like a kangaroo among the beauty

19.

I'm still Mormon the way a zoo's golden eagle
worries clipped wings, and also the way a rewilded wolf
tastes captivity in her one chipped tooth

20.

I'm Mormon the way skunk-smell lingers,
long after the boys lure it into the girls' cabin,
slam a wire cage over its surprise, its vicious

21.

hiss-and-spray, the way the stinkcloud
clings to hair, to skin, to grandmother's yellow patchwork
quilt the girl should've left home but brought for comfort
and how could she know boys could be so mean

22.

I'm Mormon the way ham hock soup is still pork knuckle
is still pig, after slaughterhouse, after blood drains
and butcher's cut through bone, chopping shank

23.

from leg, metatarsal from tibia, boiling down gristle
and skin to soften the meat and beans

24.

I'm still Mormon the way scars glisten, or angiomas
cauterized from left temple
resurface elsewhere like beads of blood

25.

As the beauty berry tree purples her fruit
in the dusky bloom of autumn night

26.

As the peach tree drops its one swelling   ·
to the ground

27.

I'm Mormon the way a Baroque theater house
combusts in its special effects, gilded ceiling
giving way to open sky and an audience of rain

28.

I'm still Mormon the way an astronaut
watches from the cupola's seven windows
as sun-slit lifts the dark from earth's contours

29.

The way a tethered astronaut turns to face the deep
black of space while loving the sun
on her back, the tug of her umbilical

30.

I'm Mormon the way a student graduates in debt
to her alma mater, school of the slowest clock and endless
scripture chase, school of humdrum,

31.

hymn-hum in braided harmony, school of Wonder
Bread, passed hand to hand in chapel hush,
the paper thimbles' drop a soft percussion

32.

I'm still Mormon the way a poem is a room
and refuses the period's lock

33.

Still Mormon the way paper gives itself over to
blade and page and pen,
but remembers what it was like to have roots, thick
woody skin, lenticels, xylem,
loved by sunlight in a copse of its kin

NOTES

For more information on Ellen Jane Robbins Bailey, her three children—Sarah (Sally), MaryAnn, and Charles—and Charles's three wives, Susannah Hawkins Bailey, Johannah Adamson Bailey, and Hannah Jones Bailey, see Charles Ramsden Bailey papers, 1839–1933. (COLL MSS 53). Utah State University. Special Collections and Archives Department.

Photographs in this collection are from *Charles Ramsden Bailey: His Life and Families,* by Jay I. and Betsy W. Long (Eden Hill, 1983) and are used with permission.

"The Mormons Are Coming" and "Post-Mormons Are Leaving" are after Carole Maso's "The Intercession of Saints."

According to historical records, Joseph Smith married 30-40 women and Brigham Young married 55. In "Brigham's Wives," the women he married are listed chronologically according to marriage date. A couple of times, he married a pair of sisters.

"Missionary Work in Kanata, Canada" is set in a city in Ontario. The word "kanata" likely comes from the Huron-Iroquois word for "village" and was later inscribed on maps as "Canada" (www.canada.ca).

"Eloher" is a mash up of Elohim (the Hebrew word used in Genesis, which translates as "the gods") and the feminine third-person pronoun her.

"P-Day at the Sugar Shack" describes a p-day or preparation day. Missionaries are allowed one day out of the week for house cleaning, laundry, grocery shopping, etc. Sometimes missionaries enjoy immersing themselves in local culture on these "days off." Québec supplies roughly 70 percent of the world's maple syrup; therefore a meal at a sugar shack, or *cabane à sucre*, is usually high on visitors' must-do lists.

"Former Mormons Catechize Their Kids" weaves together narratives from many religious traditions and mythological sources, including Judeo-Christian, ancient Egyptian, ancient Greek, African, Native American, Asian, and Pacific Islander.

"Founder's Day" describes a sham battle, which has been part of Wellsville, Utah, Founder's Day celebrations since 1930. After the September 2017 sham battle, several concerned citizens gathered at Wellsville City Hall to protest. Darren Parry, chair of the Northwestern Band of the Shoshone Nation, was appointed to a committee to help decide the future of the sham battle.

"Dear May" refers to May Swenson (1913–89), born in Logan, Utah, and interred in the Logan Cemetery. She once said, ""It's not for me — religion. It seems like a redundancy for a poet."

"If Mother Braids a Waterfall" is after Sue William Silverman and Timothy Liu.

"Still Mormon" borrows phrases from Emily Dickinson and John Keats.

ACKNOWLEDGEMENTS

I am grateful to the editors of the following journals and anthologies, in which these pieces, some of them in slightly different versions, first appeared:

Amethyst Review: "We Christen the Canoe Sunday School," "May Day"

Barrelhouse: "Pon Farr"

Clover: A Literary Rag: "I Could Never Be a Jehovah's Witness"

Coffin Bell Journal: "Ode to Polygamy," "Joseph Smith's Death Mask," "Hyrum Smith's Death Mask"

Dialogue: "Stained Glass"

Exponent II Magazine: "Proselytizing by a Marian Shrine in Québec," "The Mormons are Coming"

The Fourth River: "Apples"

Hawaii Pacific Review: "Dear Grandma"

Into the Void: "Contrails," "The Mercy of Mud"

Irreantum: "Volvelle"

The Lake: "Growing Up in a Bookstore"

Literary Mama: "Hippocampus," "After the Divorce," "Dear Grandpa"

POETRY: "Study for Belief with Lines from *Star Trek: The Original Series*"

Segullah: "If Mother Braids a Waterfall," "Moses Removed His Shoes"

Sunstone Magazine: "Missionary Work in Kanata, Canada,"
"P-Day at the Sugar Shack," "Revision," "Former Mormons
Catechize Their Kids," "Still Mormon"

Thimble Magazine: "Pioneer Day"

Weave: "With Grandmother-in-Law, Museum of Florida
History"

West Texas Literary Review: "Post-Mormons Are Leaving"

Wilderness Interface Zone: "Dear Mom"

In addition, the following poems appeared in the chapbooks
Loose Threads (2010) and *Mothering* (2011), published by Flutter
Press: "Dear Charles," "Dear Susannah," and "Grandmother"

"Eloher" won first place and a *Dialogue* award for Poetic
Excellence in the A Mother Here Art and Poetry Contest.
"Heavenly Mother Has a Degree in Exterior Design," "Gods'
Harvest Dance," and "Whale Watching" were published as well
on the contest website. These four poems and "Proselytizing
by a Marian Shrine in Québec," also appear in *Dove Song:
Heavenly Mother in Mormon Poetry* (Peculiar Pages, 2018).

"Our Lord Jesus in Drag" was published in *Psaltery & Lyre.*

"The Disposal of Mormon Garments" was published and
nominated for a Pushcart Prize by *Two Cities Review* in 2017.

"Thirty-Three Reasons Why: A Partial List" was first printed in
*Baring Witness: 36 Mormon Women Talk Candidly about Love,
Sex, and Marriage*, edited by Holly Welker (University of Illinois
Press, 2016).

My thanks to all who read through this manuscript and gave me insightful feedback: Jessica Lee, Rachel Mehl, Susan Elizabeth Howe, Marilyn Bushman-Carlton, Brenda Miller, Elizabeth Vignali, Daniel Kidd, Nancy Page, and the staff at Signature Books. May your liquid gold increase and continue to sweeten the world.

For the wise editorial advice at various stages in the process of assembling these poems, I am also indebted to Bruce Beasley, Suzanne Paola, Rebecca Beardsall, Marley Simmons-Abril, Kathryn Kendall-Weed, Jenny Lara, Fallon Sullivan, Mike Oliphant, Rosemary Engelfried, Megan Spiegel, Jennifer Bullis, Jory Mickelson, Brent Beal, Heather Olsen Beal, Elizabeth Cranford Garcia, Kami Westhoff, Dee Dee Chapman, Cindy Hollenbeck, Kelly Magee, Amy Anderson Guerra, Tyler Chadwick, Trish Kc Buel Wheeldon, Steven L. Peck, and Kim Taylor. May your hives ever hum and overbrim.

MORE POETRY FROM SIGNATURE

Salt
Susan Elizabeth Howe

paperback: $19.95
ebook: $6.00

**To the Mormon Newlyweds
Who Thought the Bellybutton
Was Somehow Involved**
Deja Earley

paperback: $19.95
ebook: $6.00

Owning the Moon
Linda Sillitoe

paperback: $22.95
ebook: $6.00

Some Love
Alex Caldiero

paperback: $17.95
ebook: $6.00